BASIC SKILLS

HAL LEONARD STUDENT PIA[NO]

Scales, Patte[rns] and Improvs

Book 1

Improvisations, Five-Finger Patterns, I–V7–I Chords and Arpeggios

TABLE OF CONTENTS

Book
ISBN 978-1-4234-4214-1

Book/CD
ISBN 978-1-4234-4217-2

HAL•LEONARD®
CORPORATION
7777 W. BLUEMOUND RD. P.O. BOX 13819 MILWAUKEE, WI 53213

In Australia contact:
Hal Leonard Australia Pty. Ltd.
4 Lentara Court
Cheltenham, Victoria, 3192 Australia
Email: ausadmin@halleonard.com.au

Visit Hal Leonard Online at
www.halleonard.com

A NOTE TO STUDENTS

Dear Piano Students,

Scales, Patterns, and Improvs presents the building blocks of music: scales, chords, arpeggios, and melodies. You will encounter them everywhere in music, so it pays to know how to play them! Daily practice of five-finger patterns, cadences, and arpeggios will help you strengthen the connection between the movement you make and the sound you create.

Playing the piano is a physical activity that uses your whole body. To make music, your eyes, ears, fingers, arms, and body work together.

- Become comfortable with the look, feel and sound of each five-finger pattern.

- Study the way the pattern looks on the keyboard. Each one appears in the Keyboard Charts beginning on page 46.

- Let your teacher show you how your fingers and arms will look when you place them in the proper five-finger position.

- Enjoy the sound of the pattern. Improvise a melody as your teacher or the CD plays an accompaniment.

- Master each five-finger pattern, cadence, and arpeggio by playing it several times. When each one feels secure, play along with the CD accompaniment. The recordings will train your ear and help you play each technical pattern evenly and musically.

- Put it all together! Play the folk song or etude for each key. When you can play each one well with the accompaniment, learn the additional skills of transposing and playing from a lead line.

Best wishes!

Barbara Kreader   *Fred Kern*   *Phillip Keveren*   *Mona Rejino*

UNIT 1

C MAJOR

IMPROVISATION (IMPROV) IN C MAJOR

Place both hands in the C Major five-finger pattern. As your teacher plays the accompaniment below, improvise a melody playing hands separately or together.

C MAJOR FIVE-FINGER PATTERN

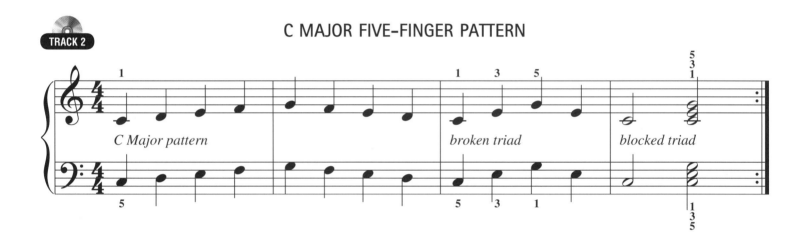

C MAJOR CADENCE I–V7–I

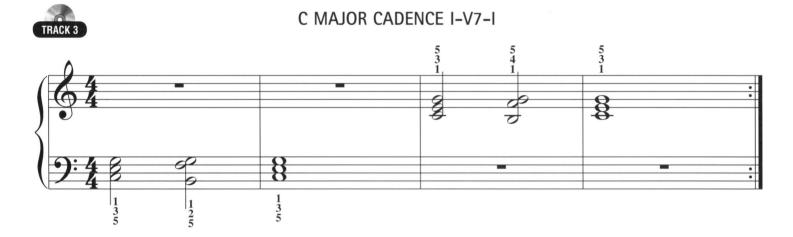

C MAJOR ARPEGGIO

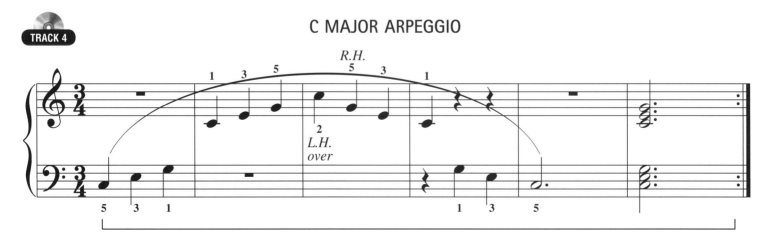

PATTERNS

Play *See-Saw* as a duet either with your teacher playing the Improv accompaniment on page 4 or with .

SEE-SAW

Gently swaying (♩ = 120)

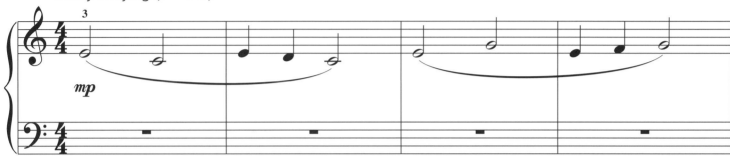

mp

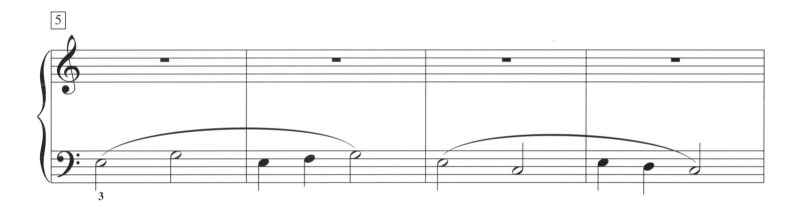

contrary motion

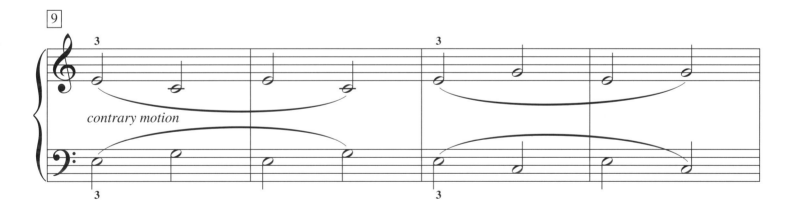

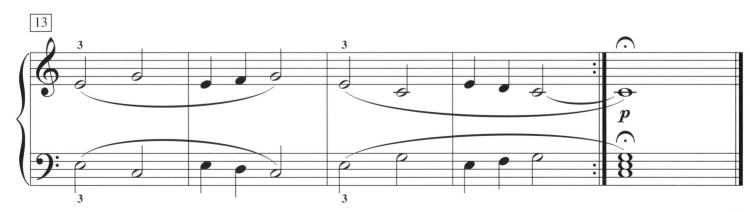

p

C MINOR

IMPROVISATION (IMPROV) IN C MINOR

Place both hands in the C Minor five-finger pattern. As your teacher plays the accompaniment below, improvise a melody playing hands separately or together.

TRACK 5

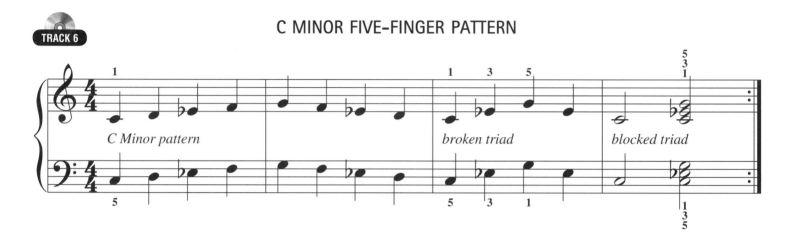

TRACK 6

C MINOR FIVE-FINGER PATTERN

C Minor pattern   *broken triad*   *blocked triad*

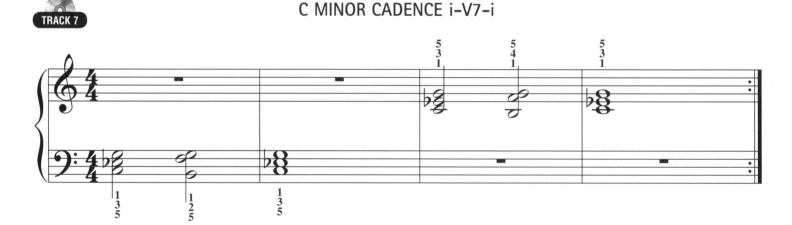

TRACK 7

C MINOR CADENCE i–V7–i

TRACK 8

C MINOR ARPEGGIO

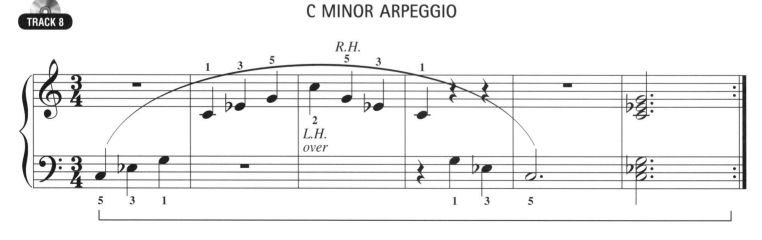

READING

1. Follow these steps before playing *Folk Song*.

   • Observe clef signs and find where to place your hands.

   • Notice the meter and rhythm; review how to count it.

   • Study the intervals and identify repeated notes, 2nds, 3rds and 5ths.

2. Play *Folk Song* as a duet either with your teacher playing the Improv accompaniment or with .

FOLK SONG

G MAJOR

IMPROVISATION (IMPROV) IN G MAJOR

Place both hands in the G Major five-finger pattern. As your teacher plays the accompaniment below, improvise a melody playing hands separately or together.

TRACK 9

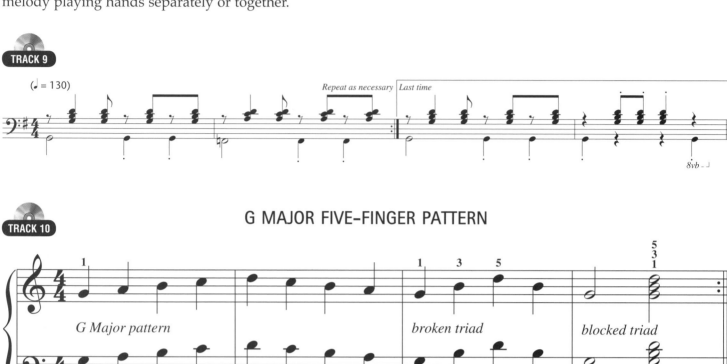

G MAJOR FIVE-FINGER PATTERN

TRACK 10

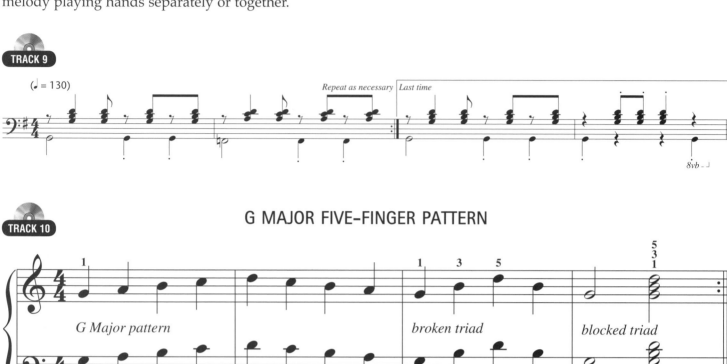

G MAJOR CADENCE I–V7–I

TRACK 11

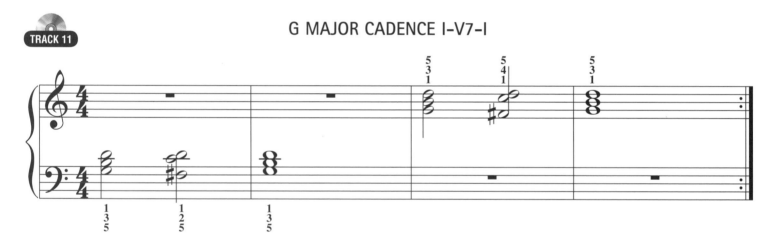

G MAJOR ARPEGGIO

TRACK 12

CHORD SYMBOLS

1. Play *Frère Jacques* with the G Major Improv accompaniment.

2. Notice that the ending of *Frère Jacques* uses the I-V7-I cadence to the words, "Wake up now!" In G Major, the chord symbol for the I chord is "G" and the chord symbol for the V7 chord is "D7." Chord symbols are usually written above each chord.

TRACK 9

FRÈRE JACQUES

Folk Song

G MINOR

IMPROVISATION (IMPROV) IN G MINOR

Place both hands in the G Minor five-finger pattern. As your teacher plays the accompaniment below, improvise a melody playing hands separately or together.

TRACK 13

G MINOR FIVE-FINGER PATTERN

TRACK 14

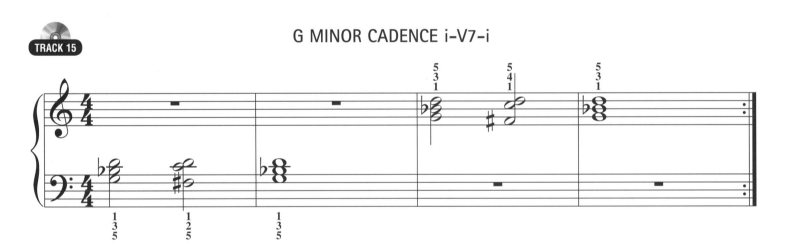

G Minor pattern

broken triad

blocked triad

G MINOR CADENCE i–V7–i

TRACK 15

G MINOR ARPEGGIO

TRACK 16

R.H.

L.H.
over

READING & TRANSPOSING

1. Play *Swedish Lullaby* with the G Minor Improv accompaniment.

SWEDISH LULLABY

Hermann Berens, Op. 62, No. 22
Adapted by Fred Kern

2. Transpose *Swedish Lullaby* by playing the piece in C Minor. Place your hands in the C Minor pattern and keep the rhythms and intervals the same.

F MAJOR

IMPROVISATION (IMPROV) IN F MAJOR

Place both hands in the F Major five-finger pattern. As your teacher plays the accompaniment below, improvise a melody playing hands separately or together.

TRACK 17

F MAJOR FIVE-FINGER PATTERN

TRACK 18

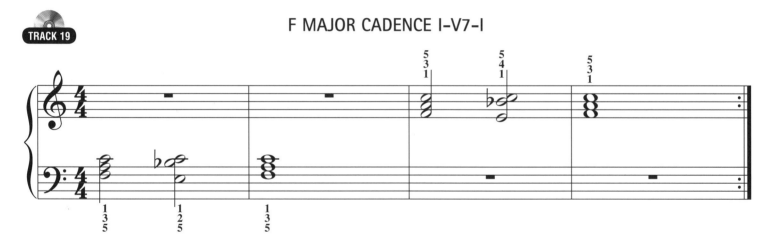

F MAJOR CADENCE I–V7–I

TRACK 19

F MAJOR ARPEGGIO

TRACK 20

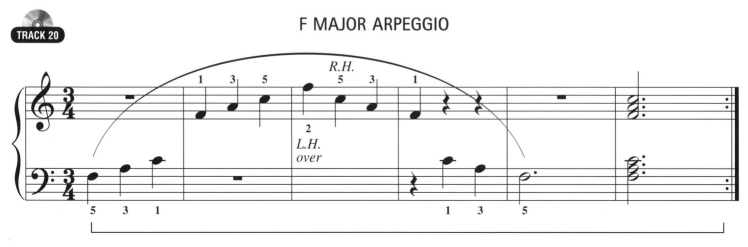

PATTERNS

Play *Rock It* with the F Major Improv accompaniment.

TRACK 17

ROCK IT

Phillip Keveren

Rock (♩ = 130)

F MINOR

IMPROVISATION (IMPROV) IN F MINOR

Place both hands in the F Minor five-finger pattern. As your teacher plays the accompaniment below, improvise a melody playing hands separately or together.

TRACK 21

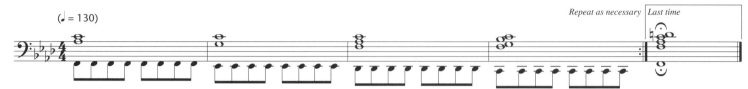

F MINOR FIVE-FINGER PATTERN

TRACK 22

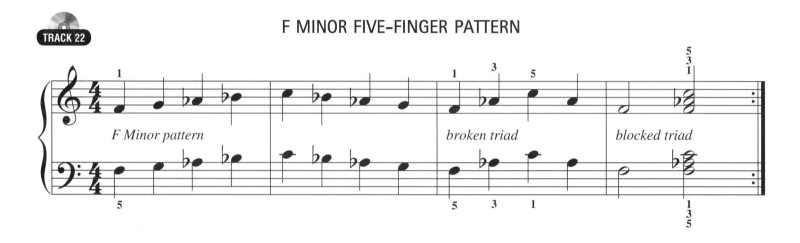

F Minor pattern   *broken triad*   *blocked triad*

F MINOR CADENCE i–V7–i

TRACK 23

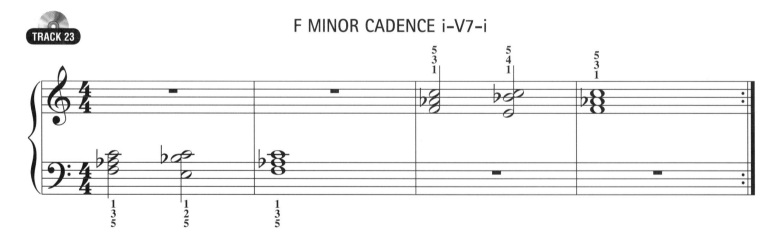

F MINOR ARPEGGIO

TRACK 24

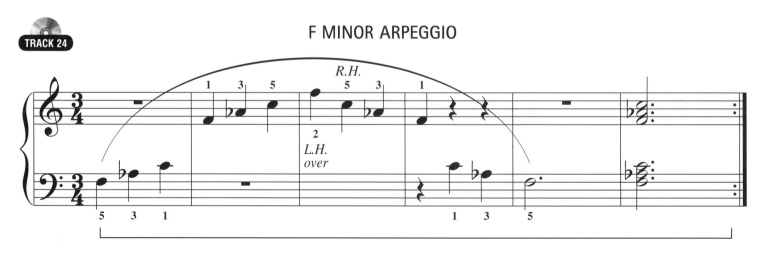

14

Play *Spy Guy* with the F Minor Improv accompaniment.

TRACK 21

SPY GUY

Slyly (♩ = 130)

Phillip Keveren

UNIT 2

D MAJOR

IMPROVISATION (IMPROV) IN D MAJOR

Place both hands in the D Major five-finger pattern. As your teacher plays the accompaniment below, improvise a melody playing hands separately or together.

TRACK 25

TRACK 26

D MAJOR FIVE-FINGER PATTERN

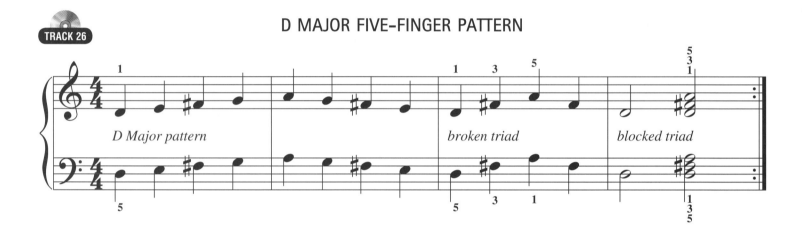

D Major pattern   *broken triad*   *blocked triad*

TRACK 27

D MAJOR CADENCE I–V7–I

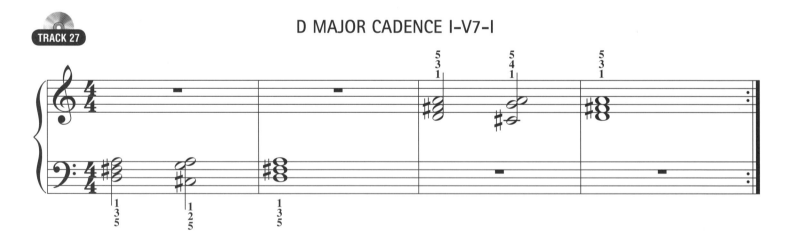

TRACK 28

D MAJOR ARPEGGIO

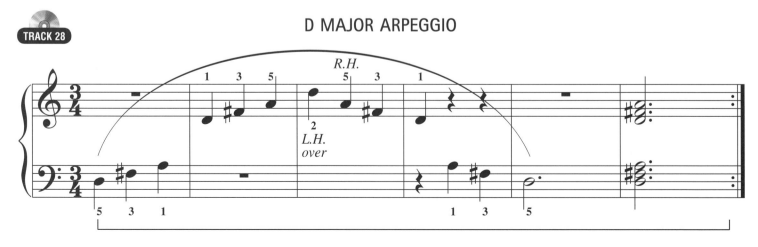

16

READING & TRANSPOSING

1. Play *A Spring Stroll* with the D Major Improv accompaniment.

A SPRING STROLL

Phillip Keveren

2. Transpose *A Spring Stroll* by playing the piece in C Major. Place your hands in the C Major pattern and keep the rhythms and intervals the same.

D MINOR

IMPROVISATION (IMPROV) IN D MINOR

Place both hands in the D Minor five-finger pattern. As your teacher plays the accompaniment below, improvise a melody playing hands separately or together.

D MINOR FIVE-FINGER PATTERN

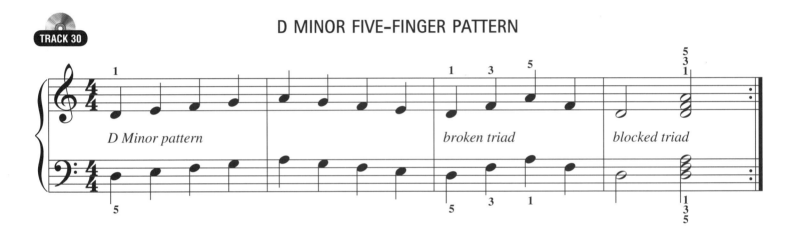

D MINOR CADENCE i–V7–i

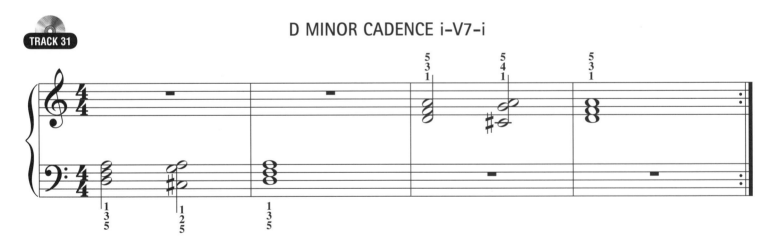

D MINOR ARPEGGIO

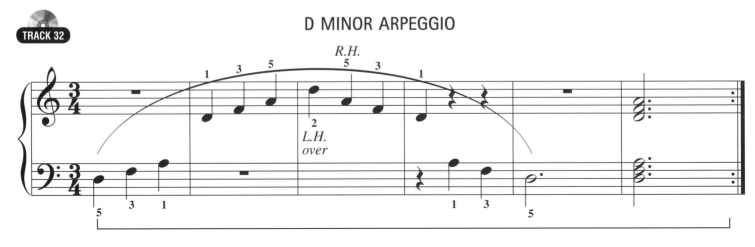

READING & TRANSPOSING

1. Play *Erie Canal* with the D Minor Improv accompaniment.

ERIE CANAL

Flowing (♩ = 120)

2. Transpose *Erie Canal* to the C Minor five-finger pattern two octaves higher than the original as your teacher plays the accompaniment below.

Accompaniment for Transposition in C Minor (*Student plays two octaves higher.*)

A MAJOR

IMPROVISATION (IMPROV) IN A MAJOR

Place both hands in the A Major five-finger pattern. As your teacher plays the accompaniment below, improvise a melody playing hands separately or together.

TRACK 33

A MAJOR FIVE-FINGER PATTERN

TRACK 34

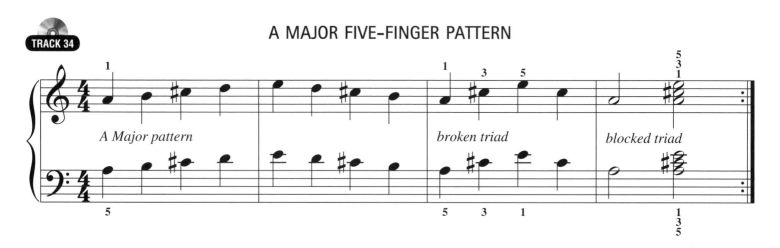

A Major pattern   *broken triad*   *blocked triad*

A MAJOR CADENCE I–V7–I

TRACK 35

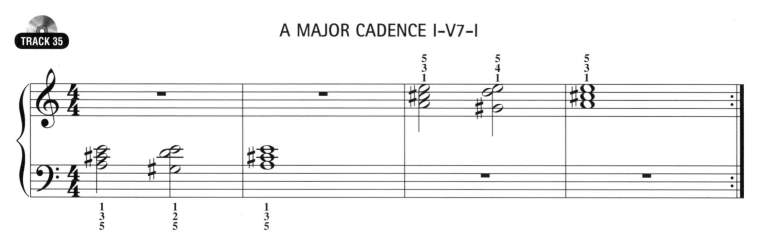

A MAJOR ARPEGGIO

TRACK 36

20

LEAD LINES

1. Play *Ode to Joy* with the A Major Improv accompaniment.

TRACK 33

ODE TO JOY

A Lead Line of a piece consists of the melody and the chords written in letters above the tune.
1. Practice the I-V7-I / A-E7-A chords on the previous page.
2. Create an accompaniment with your left hand using the chord symbols above the melody.
3. Combine the right-hand melody with the left-hand accompaniment.

A MINOR

IMPROVISATION (IMPROV) IN A MINOR

Place both hands in the A Minor five-finger pattern. As your teacher plays the accompaniment below, improvise a melody playing hands separately or together.

A MINOR FIVE-FINGER PATTERN

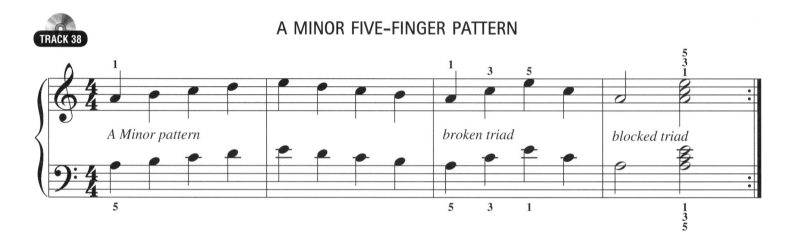

A MINOR CADENCE i–V7–i

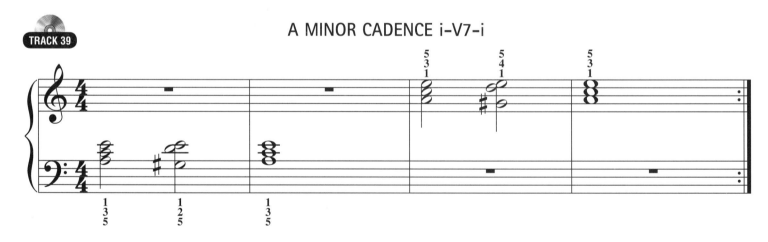

A MINOR ARPEGGIO

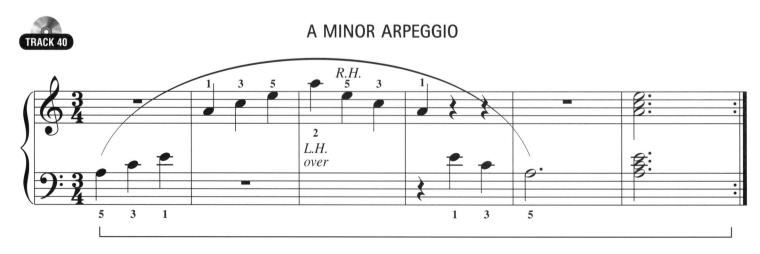

1. Play *Jazz Cat* with the A Minor Improv accompaniment.

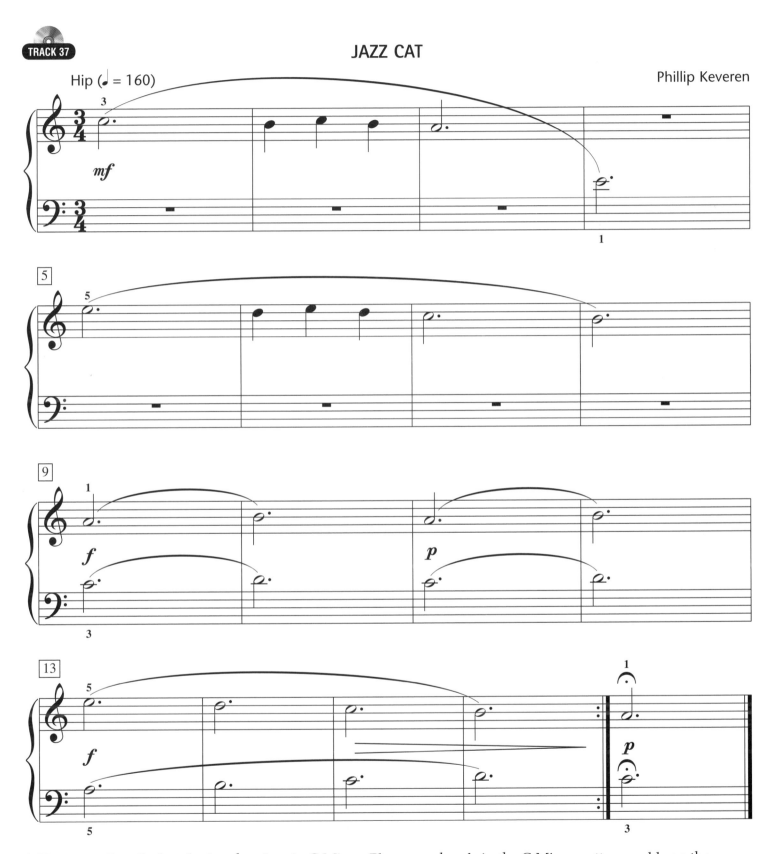

TRACK 37

JAZZ CAT

Phillip Keveren

2. Transpose *Jazz Cat* by playing the piece in G Minor. Place your hands in the G Minor pattern and keep the rhythms and intervals the same.

E MAJOR

IMPROVISATION (IMPROV) IN E MAJOR

Place both hands in the E Major five-finger pattern. As your teacher plays the accompaniment below, improvise a melody playing hands separately or together.

TRACK 41

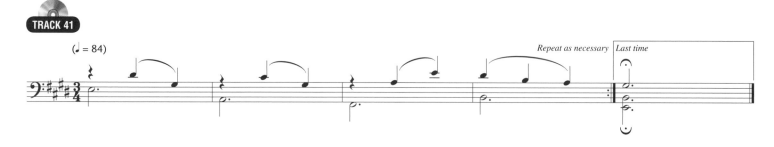

E MAJOR FIVE-FINGER PATTERN

TRACK 42

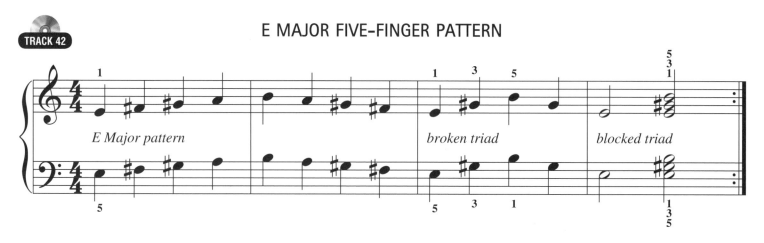

E Major pattern   *broken triad*   *blocked triad*

E MAJOR CADENCE I–V7–I

TRACK 43

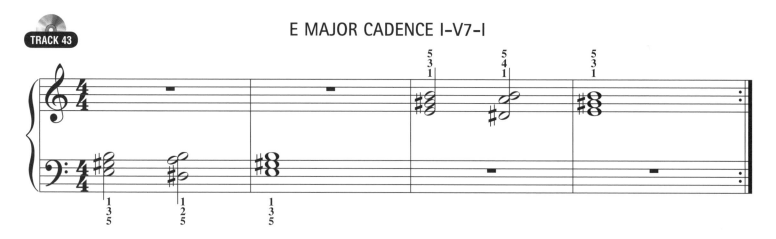

E MAJOR ARPEGGIO

TRACK 44

Play *Measure by Measure* with the E Major Improv accompaniment.

TRACK 41

MEASURE BY MEASURE

Fred Kern

Gently (♩ = 84)

E MINOR

IMPROVISATION (IMPROV) IN E MINOR

Place both hands in the E Minor five-finger pattern. As your teacher plays the accompaniment below, improvise a melody playing hands separately or together.

TRACK 45

TRACK 46

E MINOR FIVE-FINGER PATTERN

E Minor pattern   *broken triad*   *blocked triad*

TRACK 47

E MINOR CADENCE i–V7–i

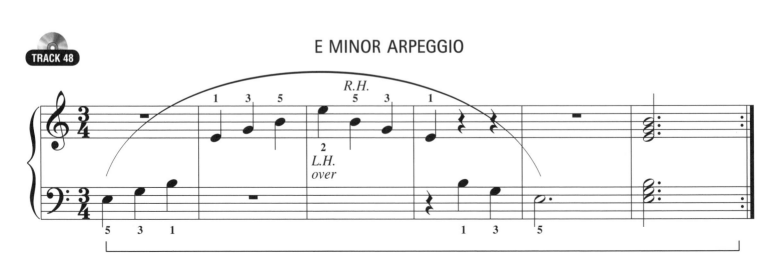

TRACK 48

E MINOR ARPEGGIO

READING & TRANSPOSING

1. Play *Melody* with the E Minor Improv accompaniment.

MELODY

TRACK 45

Hermann Berens, Op. 62, No. 14
Adapted by Fred Kern

2. Transpose *Melody* to the D Minor five-finger pattern two octaves higher as your teacher plays the accompaniment below.

Accompaniment for Transposition in D Minor (*Student plays two octaves higher.*)

UNIT 3

D♭ MAJOR

IMPROVISATION (IMPROV) IN D♭ MAJOR

Place both hands in the D♭ Major five-finger pattern. As your teacher plays the accompaniment below, improvise a melody playing hands separately or together.

D♭ MAJOR FIVE-FINGER PATTERN

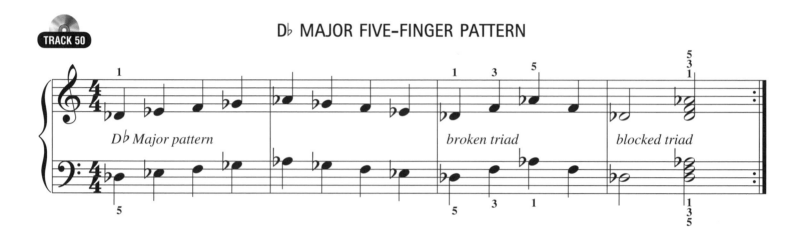

D♭ MAJOR CADENCE I–V7–I

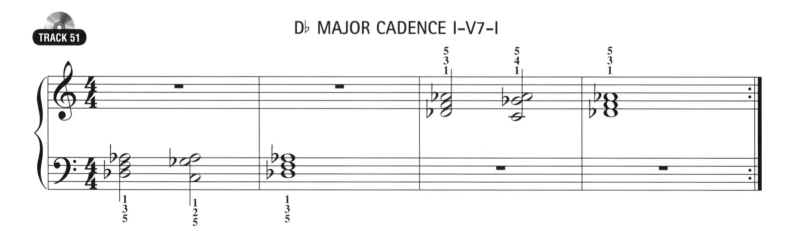

D♭ MAJOR ARPEGGIO

LEAD LINES

1. Play the right-hand melody of *French Tune* with the Db Major accompaniment.
2. Create an accompaniment with your left hand using the chord symbols above the melody. If no chord symbol is indicated, repeat the chord of the previous measure.
3. Combine the right-hand melody with the left-hand accompaniment and play *French Tune* as a solo.

FRENCH TUNE

C♯ MINOR

IMPROVISATION (IMPROV) IN C♯ MINOR

Place both hands in the C♯ Minor five-finger pattern. As your teacher plays the accompaniment below, improvise a melody playing hands separately or together.

TRACK 53

TRACK 54

C♯ MINOR FIVE-FINGER PATTERN

C♯ Minor pattern   *broken triad*   *blocked triad*

TRACK 55

C♯ MINOR CADENCE i–V7–i

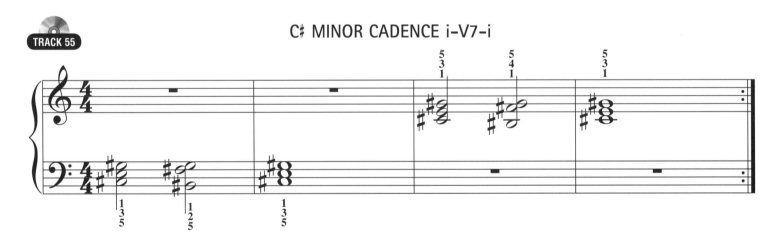

TRACK 56

C♯ MINOR ARPEGGIO

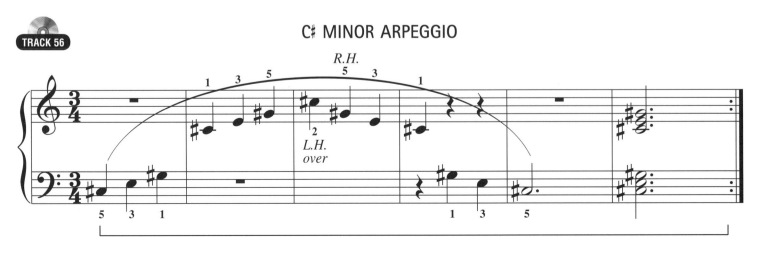

CHORDAL ACCOMPANIMENTS

1. Play *Tambourine Tune* with the C♯ Minor accompaniment.

2. Using the Roman numerals as a guide, write the correct i and V7 chords in whole notes in the gray boxes.

3. Combine the right-hand melody with the left-hand accompaniment and play *Tambourine Tune* as a solo.

TAMBOURINE TUNE

A♭ MAJOR

IMPROVISATION (IMPROV) IN A♭ MAJOR

Place both hands in the A♭ Major five-finger pattern. As your teacher plays the accompaniment below, improvise a melody playing hands separately or together.

TRACK 57

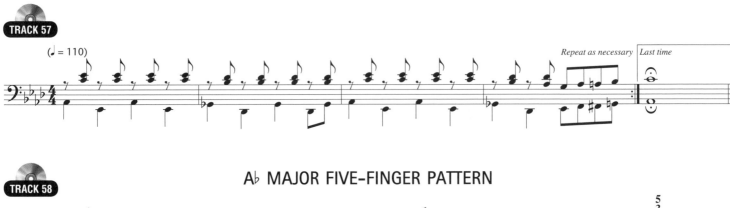

A♭ MAJOR FIVE-FINGER PATTERN

TRACK 58

A♭ MAJOR CADENCE I–V7–I

TRACK 59

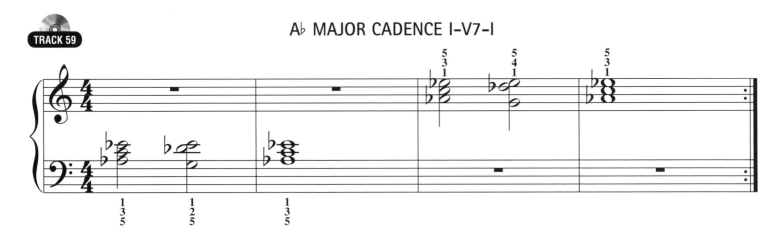

A♭ MAJOR ARPEGGIO

TRACK 60

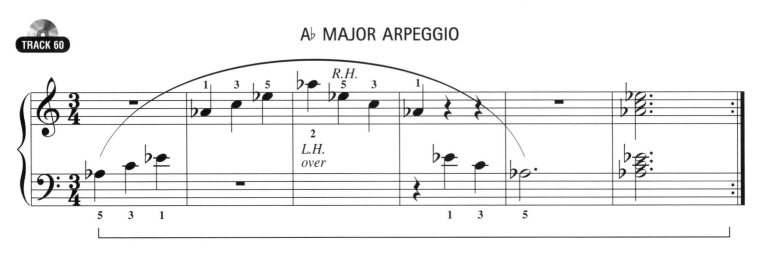

PATTERNS

Play *Line Up* with the A♭ Major Improv accompaniment.

LINE UP

Fred Kern

Play both hands 8va throughout.
Spirited (♩ = 110)

IMPROVISATION (IMPROV) IN A♭ MINOR

Place both hands in the A♭ Minor five-finger pattern. As your teacher plays the accompaniment below, improvise a melody playing hands separately or together.

TRACK 61

A♭ MINOR FIVE-FINGER PATTERN

TRACK 62

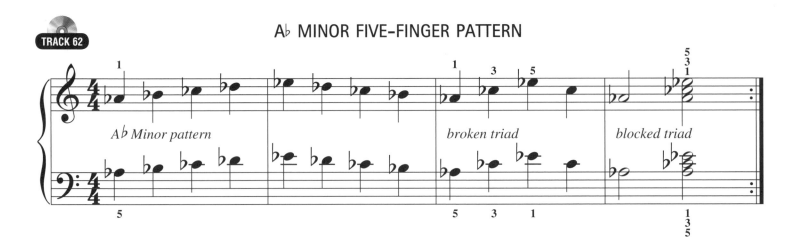

A♭ MINOR CADENCE i–V7–i

TRACK 63

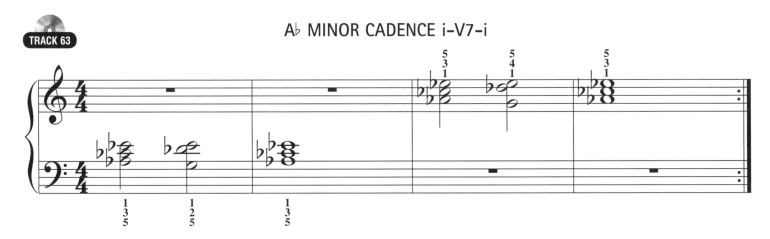

A♭ MINOR ARPEGGIO

TRACK 64

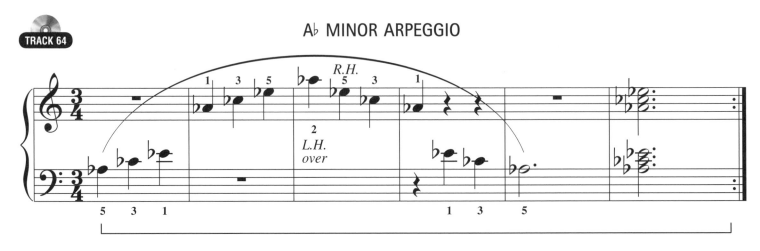

CHORDAL ACCOMPANIMENTS

1. Play the melody of *Round Dance* with the A♭ Minor accompaniment.

2. Using the Roman numerals as a guide, write the correct i and V7 chords in whole notes in the gray boxes.

3. Combine the melody with the accompaniment and play *Round Dance* as a solo.

ROUND DANCE

Hungarian Folk Tune

E♭ MAJOR

IMPROVISATION (IMPROV) IN E♭ MAJOR

Place both hands in the E♭ Major five-finger pattern. As your teacher plays the accompaniment below, improvise a melody playing hands separately or together.

TRACK 65

TRACK 66

E♭ MAJOR FIVE-FINGER PATTERN

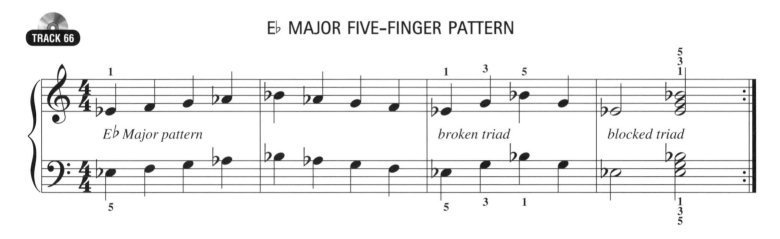

TRACK 67

E♭ MAJOR CADENCE I–V7–I

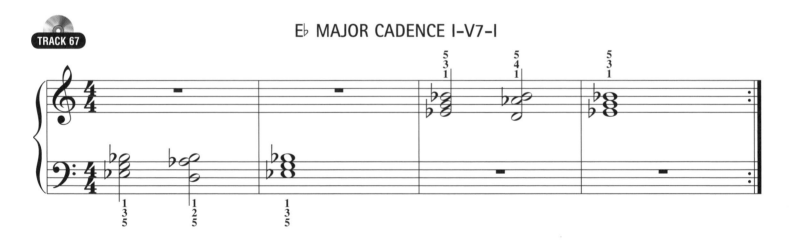

TRACK 68

E♭ MAJOR ARPEGGIO

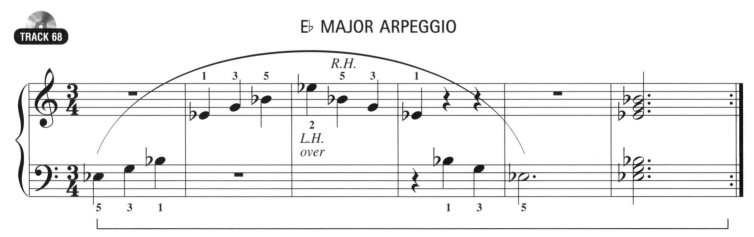

CHORDAL ACCOMPANIMENTS

1. Play *Pop! Goes the Weasel* with the E♭ Major accompaniment.

2. Using the Roman numerals as a guide, write the correct I and V7 chords in dotted half notes in the gray boxes.

3. Combine the melody with the accompaniment and play *Pop! Goes the Weasel* as a solo.

POP! GOES THE WEASEL

E♭ MINOR

IMPROVISATION (IMPROV) IN E♭ MINOR

Place both hands in the E♭ Minor five-finger pattern. As your teacher plays the accompaniment below, improvise a melody playing hands separately or together.

TRACK 69

E♭ MINOR FIVE-FINGER PATTERN

TRACK 70

E♭ MINOR CADENCE i–V7–i

TRACK 71

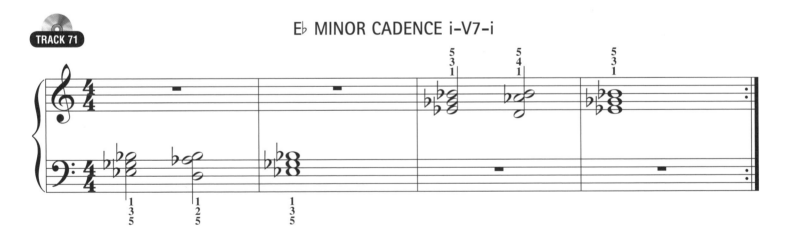

E♭ MINOR ARPEGGIO

TRACK 72

PATTERNS

Play *Star to Star* with the E♭ Minor Improv accompaniment.

STAR TO STAR

Bb MAJOR

IMPROVISATION (IMPROV) IN Bb MAJOR

Place both hands in the Bb Major five-finger pattern. As your teacher plays the accompaniment below, improvise a melody playing hands separately or together.

Bb MAJOR FIVE-FINGER PATTERN

Bb MAJOR CADENCE I–V7–I

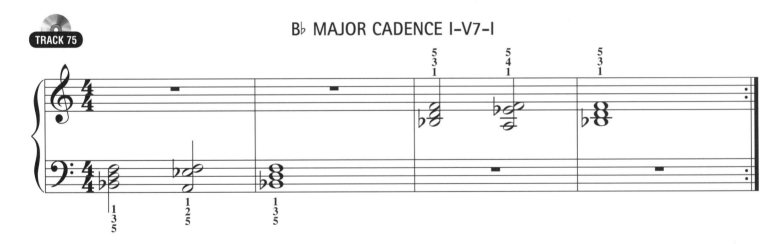

Bb MAJOR ARPEGGIO

B♭ MINOR

IMPROVISATION (IMPROV) IN B♭ MINOR

Place both hands in the B♭ Minor five-finger pattern. As your teacher plays the accompaniment below, improvise a melody playing hands separately or together.

B♭ MINOR FIVE-FINGER PATTERN

B♭ Minor pattern   *broken triad*   *blocked triad*

B♭ MINOR CADENCE i–V7–i

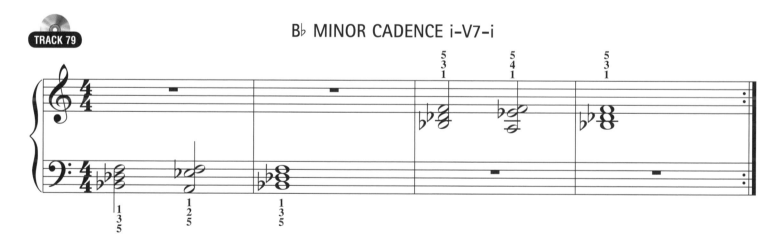

B♭ MINOR ARPEGGIO

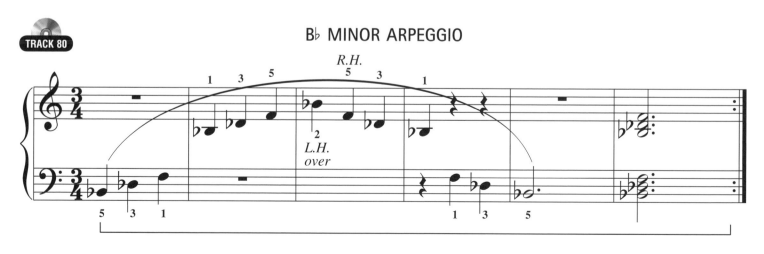

B MAJOR

IMPROVISATION (IMPROV) IN B MAJOR

Place both hands in the B Major five-finger pattern. As your teacher plays the accompaniment below, improvise a melody playing hands separately or together.

TRACK 81

B MAJOR FIVE-FINGER PATTERN

TRACK 82

B Major pattern *broken triad* *blocked triad*

B MAJOR CADENCE I–V7–I

TRACK 83

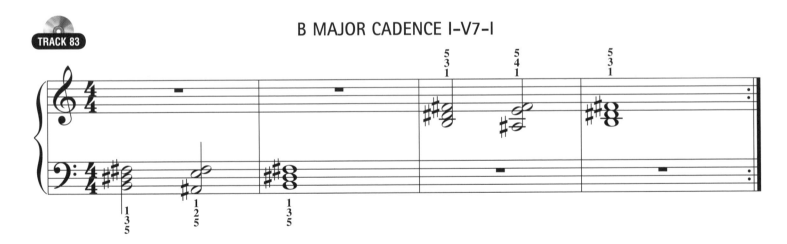

B MAJOR ARPEGGIO

TRACK 84

B MINOR

IMPROVISATION (IMPROV) IN B MINOR

Place both hands in the B Minor five-finger pattern. As your teacher plays the accompaniment below, improvise a melody playing hands separately or together.

TRACK 85

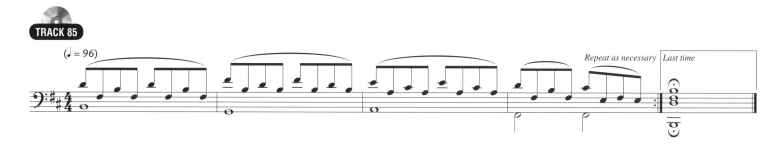

B MINOR FIVE-FINGER PATTERN

TRACK 86

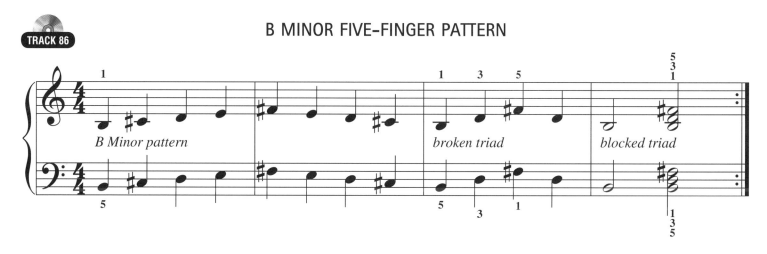

B MINOR CADENCE i–V7–i

TRACK 87

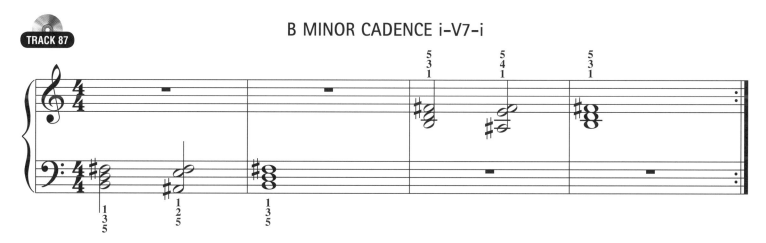

B MINOR ARPEGGIO

TRACK 88

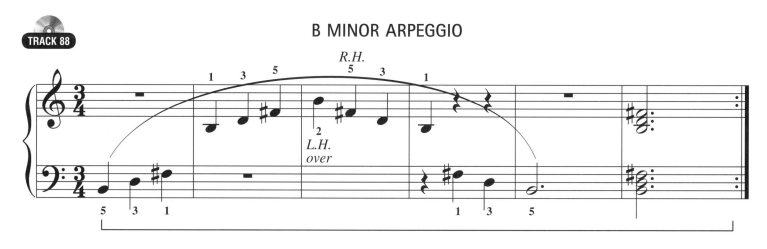

F♯ MAJOR

IMPROVISATION (IMPROV) IN F♯ MAJOR

Place both hands in the F♯ Major five-finger pattern. As your teacher plays the accompaniment below, improvise a melody playing hands separately or together.

TRACK 89

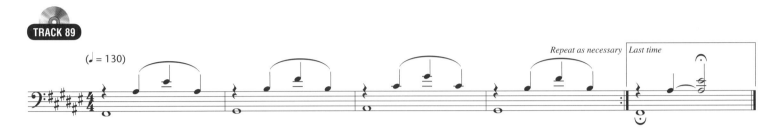

F♯ MAJOR FIVE-FINGER PATTERN

TRACK 90

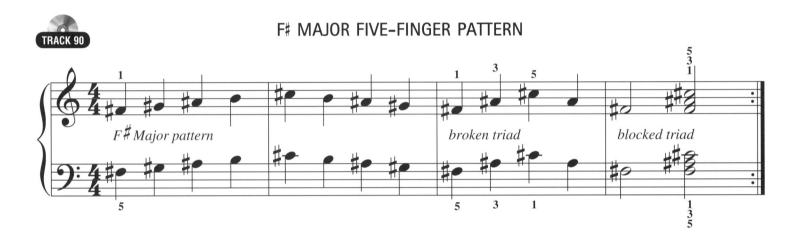

F♯ MAJOR CADENCE I–V7–I

TRACK 91

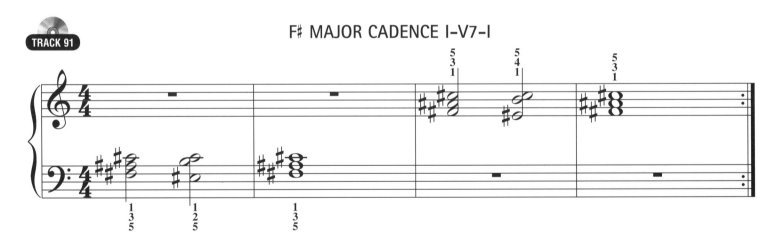

F♯ MAJOR ARPEGGIO

TRACK 92

F♯ MINOR

IMPROVISATION (IMPROV) IN F♯ MINOR

Place both hands in the F♯ Minor five-finger pattern. As your teacher plays the accompaniment below, improvise a melody playing hands separately or together.

TRACK 93

F♯ MINOR FIVE-FINGER PATTERN

TRACK 94

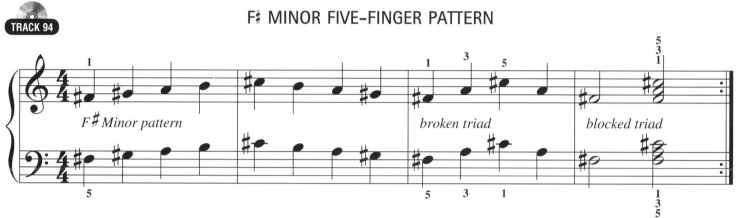

F♯ MINOR CADENCE i–V7–i

TRACK 95

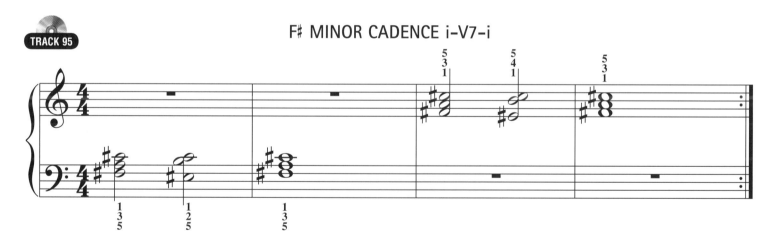

F♯ MINOR ARPEGGIO

TRACK 96

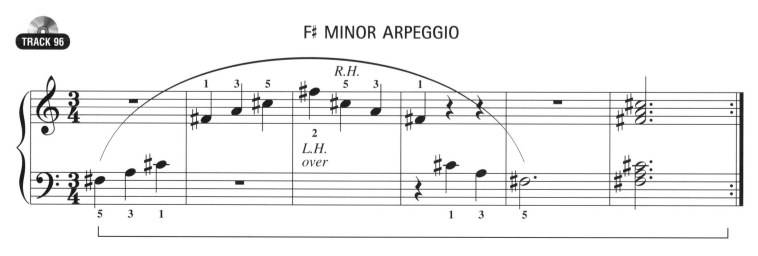

KEYBOARD CHARTS

C Major pattern

I

V⁷

C Minor pattern

i

V⁷

G Major pattern

I

V⁷

G Minor pattern

i

V⁷

F Major pattern

I

V⁷

F Minor pattern

i

V⁷

D Major pattern

I

V⁷

D Minor pattern

i

V⁷

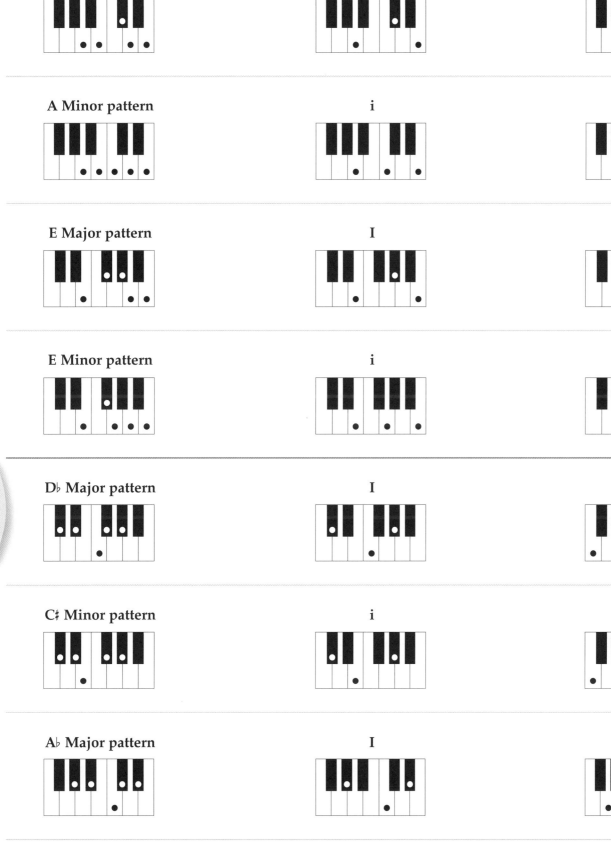

A Major pattern	I	V⁷
A Minor pattern	i	V⁷
E Major pattern	I	V⁷
E Minor pattern	i	V⁷
D♭ Major pattern	I	V⁷
C♯ Minor pattern	i	V⁷
A♭ Major pattern	I	V⁷
A♭ Minor pattern	i	V⁷

UNIT 3

47